WICCA

ESSENTIAL OILS MAGIC

A Beginner's Guide to Working with Magical Oils, with Simple Recipes and Spells

LISA CHAMBERLAIN

Wicca Essential Oils Magic

Copyright © 2017 by Lisa Chamberlain.

Published by **Chamberlain Publications (Wicca Shorts)**

ISBN-13: 978-1-912715-62-6

Disclaimer

No part of this publication may be reproduced or transmitted in any form or by any means, mechanical or electronic, including photocopying or recording, or by any information storage and retrieval system, or transmitted by email without permission in writing from the publisher.

While all attempts have been made to verify the information provided in this publication, neither the author nor the publisher assumes any responsibility for errors, omissions, or contrary interpretations of the subject matter herein.

This book is for entertainment purposes only. The views expressed are those of the author alone, and should not be taken as expert instruction or commands. The reader is responsible for his or her own actions.

Adherence to all applicable laws and regulations, including international, federal, state, and local governing professional licensing, business practices, advertising, and all other aspects of doing business in the US, Canada, or any other jurisdiction is the sole responsibility of the purchaser or reader.

Neither the author nor the publisher assumes any responsibility or liability whatsoever on the behalf of the purchaser or reader of these materials.

Any perceived slight of any individual or organization is purely unintentional.

YOUR FREE GIFT

Thank you for adding this book to your Wiccan library! To learn more, why not join Lisa's Wiccan community and get an exclusive, free spell book?

The book is a great starting point for anyone looking to try their hand at practicing magic. The ten beginner-friendly spells can help you to create a positive atmosphere within your home, protect yourself from negativity, and attract love, health, and prosperity.

Little Book of Spells is now available to read on your laptop, phone, tablet, Kindle or Nook device!

To download, simply visit the following link:

www.wiccaliving.com/bonus

GET THREE
FREE AUDIOBOOKS
FROM LISA CHAMBERLAIN

Did you know that all of Lisa's books are available in audiobook format? Best of all, you can get **three audiobooks completely free** as part of a 30-day trial with Audible.

Wicca Starter Kit contains three of Lisa's most popular books for beginning Wiccans, all in one convenient place. It's the best and easiest way to learn more about Wicca while also taking audiobooks for a spin! Simply visit:

www.wiccaliving.com/free-wiccan-audiobooks

Alternatively, *Spellbook Starter Kit* is the ideal option for building your magical repertoire using candle and color magic, crystals and mineral stones, and magical herbs. Three spellbooks —over 150 spells—are available in one free volume, here:

www.wiccaliving.com/free-spell-audiobooks

Audible members receive free audiobooks every month, as well as exclusive discounts. It's a great way to experiment and see if audiobook learning works for you.

If you're not satisfied, you can cancel anytime within the trial period. You won't be charged, and you can still keep your books!

CONTENTS

INTRODUCTION

Of all the tools and ingredients used in Wicca and other forms of Witchcraft, perhaps none are quite as intriguing and mysterious as magical oils.

The scents of myrrh and cedarwood, or perhaps a blend of lavender and clove, seem to instantly awaken something in us that's beyond our ordinary sense of smell and put us into a different frame of mind—one that is more in touch with the invisible powers of the Universe, and therefore more able to direct those powers to achieve our aims.

Since before recorded history, shamans, priests and healers used scented oils in ritual, magic and medicine. Oils were used in incense, ointments, tinctures, charms and other magical creations for almost every purpose under the Sun.

Because of their unique effects on the mind of the practitioner, botanical oils provide a direct tie between the natural physical world and the spiritual plane. As with other forms of herbal magic, the use of oils has the potential to transform lives on physical, emotional, and spiritual levels.

This book provides an overview of magical botanical oils and their use in contemporary Witchcraft. While this topic technically extends to their contribution to the making of incense, magical ointments and other creations, the focus here in this beginner's guide is on the oils themselves—both as single ingredients and as magical blends. This is in part because the full breadth of information about oils would fill up a large tome, but also because it's worth getting to know oils on their own before taking on more involved magical projects.

In Part One, we'll start with a brief look at how our spiritual forbears in the Craft used scented oils in ritual, magic and healing in ancient civilizations. We'll trace the evolution of botanical oils from their rustic beginnings to their modern incarnations in the form of essential oils, and then examine how they work on the magical level to aid us in manifestation.

In Part Two, you'll meet 13 essential oils commonly used in both healing and contemporary magic, many with histories of ritual and magical use going back for thousands of years. This selection represents a range of scents, plant types, and healing and magical properties, for a well-rounded introduction to the world of magical oils.

Part Three presents a grimoire of sorts, with detailed instructions and tips for creating your own magical blends. You'll find several blend recipes, some oil-oriented spells for you to try your hand at, and a few ideas for taking your practice further.

Finally, you'll find a table of correspondence outlining the magical properties of oils, along with their relationships to specific deities, Zodiac signs, elements and planets, for those who like to use these correspondences in their spellwork.

By the end of this guide, you will have a solid foundation to work from in your continuing education in incorporating magical oils into your practice. Enjoy the journey, and Blessed Be!

PART ONE

THE MAGICAL WORLD OF OILS

THE TRANSFORMATIVE POWER OF SCENT

Imagine walking into a pastry shop and catching the scent of flour and cinnamon, mixed with just a hint of almond and vanilla. The smell takes you straight back to your grandmother's kitchen, where as a child you watched her mixing and rolling out dough, the warmth of the oven steaming up the edges of the windows. You remember a strong feeling of love and safety, and the delightful anticipation of the delicious treats that would arrive in a short while.

You can even begin to remember the faint orange color of the wallpaper and the solid feel of the oak kitchen table, where you rested your forearms as you leaned over to watch her work. Now and then she would look up from her mixing bowls and spoons to give you a smile or a wink, dusting her flour-white hands on her ancient apron. Now the sound of her voice comes into your ears, along with memories of your childhood and the way you saw the world back in those simple times.

Then suddenly, you hear the bell on the door of the pastry shop ring. You feel a rush of cold air as the door opens and more customers enter. And just like that, you are yanked out of your childhood self in your grandmother's kitchen and returned to your present self, fully grown and standing in front of the pastry case, which you realize you have been looking at for what must have been several minutes, without actually registering any of the offerings.

Only it hasn't been several minutes—not even close. It may have felt like ages, but in reality you've just taken a vivid journey of many years and many miles in five seconds flat. And all because of a single whiff of a combination of flour, cinnamon, almond and vanilla.

Most of us can relate to this scenario in one form or another. We may not have had grandmothers who baked for us in their kitchens, but everyone has had a childhood filled with physical, emotional and sensory experiences that add up to form the memories we access from time to time as adults.

Many things can elicit a sudden, seemingly forgotten memory: music, an old movie, a drive through a former neighborhood. But of the five physical senses, nothing is more powerful a trigger than our sense of smell.

A particular smell can actually alter our state of mind, transporting us on the wings of timeless connections to places we haven't been for years or decades, stirring up strong emotions, or simply bringing about a sense of calm well-being. And new scents can actually create entirely new experiences in the mind, transporting us to new realms of thought and emotion. Indeed, the sense of smell is a powerful aspect of human life. If you doubt this, just take a look at the size and scope of the perfume industry!

Plenty of research has been done over the past century or so that explains, on a physiological level, why our sense of smell is so distinctly linked to memory and emotion. But Witches and healers have always understood that this connection is a psychic phenomenon as well.

This is what gives scented oils their potential to work powerful magic. After all, magic is all about your state of mind and your ability to focus your intention on the spiritual plane. You can have all the ritual tools, sacred herbs, and charged-up candles in the world at your disposal, but if you can't summon the necessary state of mind to send your intention confidently into the Universe, you're unlikely to get the results you seek.

This is why incense is such a key part of ritual and magic in Wiccan and other Pagan traditions—as the richly scented smoke wafts throughout the sacred space, it puts us in a frame of mind that is unconcerned, for the time being, with the mundane details of everyday life. We are more able to focus on going within, connecting with our deities, our higher selves, or whatever our belief systems recognize as the power that aids us in transforming our reality.

Scented oils provide another way of promoting this inner focus, and oils that are blended and charged specifically for magical purposes are arguably the most potent aromatic resources we can have at our disposal.

This is why Witches use them to anoint their ritual tools, their crystals, their talismans, charms and amulets, and even their own bodies. Oils provide an extra boost to magic like nothing else on Earth can. However, using this power to its fullest potential requires a willingness to really understand where it comes from. Too often, a novice Witch will acquire an oil blend or two, dutifully anoint her spell candles with it, and then put the bottle away without having any real sense of what's in it or how it was made.

Unlike crystals, herbs, and other tools and ingredients that can be held and explored directly with our hands, oils are somewhat more mysterious when we first encounter them. Of course, there's always a hint of mystery around truly magical things, but that doesn't mean we should be unaware of the contents of the substances we work with.

So in the spirit of having a solid grounding in the use of oils, we'll now explore a little bit about their origins and the evolution of their use over the centuries. Then we'll take a more in-depth look at the power inherent in botanical oils, and the role they can play in the process of magical manifestation.

OILS IN ANCIENT SPIRITUAL TRADITIONS

Fragrant oils derived from plant sources have been used for both medicinal and magical purposes since the beginning of recorded history. Of course, in the centuries before the advent of modern science, these areas of life were much more intertwined than they are now. Healing was often accomplished using herbal remedies, but these medicines were considered sacred, as they came from Nature and had their own living energies.

Indeed, most ancient cultures prized plants for their magical properties, and used them in rituals and other workings as well as in food and medicine. Among the most highly valued plants were the aromatics—plants that exude particular scents—which lent themselves to the creation of richly perfumed oils to please the people and the gods alike. Aromatics

17

were also used in the creation of incense, which consisted primarily of dried plant matter but might also include the "essence," or oil, of the plants as well.

Both oils and incense were crucial elements of religious practices in ancient cultures around the globe. The scents of trees, shrubs and grasses like cedar, lavender and palmarosa were believed to forge a connection between between the physical and the spiritual planes. Deities could be contacted through the smoke of incense, and offerings made to the gods were anointed with oils. Herbs and oils were also involved in burial rites and rituals, believed to help the recently deceased make their journey to the afterlife.

Ancient Egypt is particularly well known for this practice. Not only were their dead anointed with magical oils, but the bodies of the deceased were actually injected with them. Cedarwood, sandalwood, myrrh and rose oil, among others, were common ingredients in the embalming potions that kept the mummified remains of their loved ones preserved for millennia.

Did the Egyptians choose these oils based on a scientific understanding of their antibacterial properties? Or was their intuitive grasp of the magical energies of these sacred plants sufficient to point them in the right direction?

Whatever the case, perfumed oils were central to Egyptian religious practices at least as far back as 3000 BCE. In fact, one of the temple priests' main functions was to offer perfumes to the gods, each of which had their own special fragrance or blend, and statues of deities were anointed with oils several times a day—up to nine times on special holidays.

Due to their stores of oils, which were also used as medicines, it was common for priests to serve as physicians as well. However, it was usually only the upper classes who had access to these fragrant oils, which were so highly valued that they were kept in special ornate flasks, some of which still contained traces of their scents when they were discovered thousands of years later!

Oils were also popular in ancient Greece and Rome. The Mycenaean civilization honored their deities with them as early as the 13th century BCE, and pottery containing traces of fragrant oils was discovered at several burial sites. Several hundred years later, Aristotle developed his theory that plants have consciousness (a theory that has seen a resurgence in recent decades) which strengthened the popular belief in the magical properties of oils.

Along with honoring their deities, the Greeks anointed their own bodies with scented oils in order to please the gods. The Greeks obtained much of their knowledge about the composition and use of oils from the Egyptians, but did not emulate the restriction

19

of their use to the wealthy—all classes of Greek society had access to oils.

Likewise in Rome, the use of oils was widespread, and not just for medicinal and spiritual purposes, but for all aspects of life. The Romans scented just about everything, from their clothes to their entire surroundings, including public baths and fountains, until the available supplies of plant life that created the oils was nearly wiped out, and they had to scale back a little.

Other ancient Old World cultures using plant-based oils included the Hebrews, Babylonians and Sumerians, as well as the Chinese, the Hindus, and many tribes in Persia and Arabia. Over the centuries of trade and travel, oils eventually made their way into the lands that came to be known as Europe, where perfumery flourished until the fall of the Roman Empire and the advent of the Dark Ages.

It took several centuries for oils to make a comeback on the Continent, but eventually the perfume trade was back up and running. The spiritual and medicinal properties of oils were also noticed by at least some clever people, who used frankincense, pine, and other oils to keep away the "evil spirits" of the black plague.

However, scented oils soon faced another adversary: the Christian Church. In their quest for total domination over European culture, Church authorities discouraged the use of oils as "earthly pleasures." This ultimately became a prohibition that was used as a weapon during the witch-hunts of the 16th and 17th centuries. Possession of scented oils was now considered evidence of witchcraft, which should come as no surprise to the modern Witch who makes ample use of these magical substances!

A MODERN RESURGENCE

Over the next few centuries, developments in science and industry led to a near-total disappearance of magic and the Craft, and the few who still practiced these traditions did so in secrecy. Chemically-based medicines replaced most natural remedies, and by the 20th century natural fragrances were all but eclipsed by synthetic imitations, which were cheaper and easier to produce.

However, natural oils didn't fall completely out of use. Although they were largely under the radar of Western mainstream society, these substances continued to be studied for their healing properties, largely by European doctors and chemists. It was a French chemist named René-Maurice Gattefossé who coined the term "aromatherapy" in the 1920s, after healing chemical burns on his hands with lavender oil. His book "Aromatherapie" was the first modern work on the medicinal properties of what we now call "essential oils."

Today, essential oils are becoming more and more widely available as interest in aromatherapy is gaining the attention of mainstream society. And while the production of these oils is largely for the purposes of alternative medicine and cosmetic applications, Witches are definitely beneficiaries of the aromatherapy "boom." In past decades, essential oils would have been nonexistent or at least very hard to come by, but there is now a wide selection available to Witches who wish to work with natural, rather than synthetic, ingredients in their spellwork.

THE EVOLUTION OF MAGICAL OILS

Although the use of oils in ritual and magic is an age-old tradition, it's worth understanding that the oils we work with today are not physically the same as those our ancestors revered. Furthermore, we have a much wider variety of natural oils at our disposal, from magical plants found all over the globe, than our forbears had access to.

Yet we're also more removed, by and large, from the process of making magical oils than ancient cultures were. Many Witches make their own blends, of course, but the ingredients in those blends are derived from manufacturing processes that most of us are not likely to be adept at! Nonetheless, we can get a clearer sense of what natural, botanical oils are, and where they come from, by taking a brief look at how they evolved over time.

In the very ancient world, oils and fats derived from olives, sesame seeds, animals and other sources were used as "carriers" for plant materials. These included leaves, flowers, barks, resins and gums from fragrant trees, shrubs and grasses. The ingredients were chopped, pressed, and heated in the oils, which absorbed their scent.

The labor-intensive process made perfumed oils a precious commodity, yet they were far less potent than the essential oils we have today. Some of the most commonly used oils in these earliest societies were frankincense, myrrh, and cinnamon. These plants were highly potent in terms of transferring their fragrance to the carrier oil.

Eventually, the process of steam distillation was discovered and refined, which enabled the processing of a wider range of plants and eliminated the need for carrier oils. Now the plant materials were placed into a container over heated water, so that the steam would draw out the essence, which would then condense back into liquid form, creating the "essential oil." These were more potent in their scent and, many would argue, their magical power, since the natural energies of the plant were far more concentrated by this process.

The origins of the distillation process are unknown, but archeologists have found evidence on Cyprus and in northern India that suggests it goes back at least 4,000 to 5,000 years. But it wasn't until the 11th century AD that the technology we base our present-day processes on was invented by a Persian physician and mystic known as Avicenna. His method eventually led to the ability to produce rose essential oil, and to a wider interest in plant-based oils in general.

Other methods that arose as technology evolved included pressing citrus oils from the peel of the fruit, such as bergamot and lemon, and extraction, which allowed for more delicate, less inherently oil-producing flowers to be processed into fragrant oils. Thus, over time a wider and wider range of magical oils has become available.

Furthermore, trade has become global, bringing previously unknown oils like vetiver and ylang-ylang from Asia to the West. Indeed, we've come a long way from having just a handful of scents available for our spellwork!

This is one of many ways in which magic and ritual practice has changed over the millennia, and for some may even seem to be a total departure from traditional magic, which is still centered around the older oils in Western history like frankincense and cedarwood.

While more "orthodox" Witches might choose to stay entirely faithful to these traditional oils as a way of staying connected with the old ways, many eclectic Witches and Pagans have delighted in experimenting with newer options such as niaouli, peach and wisteria, branching out into new realms of possibility for magical manifestation.

OILS AND THE MAGICAL PROCESS

Although the variety of botanical essential oils available to the 21st-century Witch is certainly a blessing for our magical practice, the real reason that oils have become so widely accessible is the explosion of interest in aromatherapy over the past few decades.

As this ancient healing method gains more respect in mainstream society, even convincing some Western medical practitioners to incorporate it into their practices, we are seeing essential oils crop up in all kinds of places, including health food stores and even some pharmacy chains. Used in massage therapy, cold and flu remedies, and anxiety relief techniques, just to name a few examples, oils have truly made a resurgence in our modern times.

Happily, Witches can now take advantage of the abundance of these natural magical tools without having to worry about religious authorities raiding their cupboards!

SCENT, BIOLOGY AND MAGIC

One particularly effective use of essential oils is in promoting relaxation and emotional balance. These are goals anyone would benefit from achieving, but for magical practice, a centered state of mind is a necessity.

Putting a few drops of certain oils in a hot bath, an oil burner, or a diffuser can make a very noticeable difference in your state of mind, whether you're planning to do some spellwork or simply want to unwind after a long day. And many people find that the consistent use of this kind of aromatherapy—for example, burning lavender oil every evening for several days or weeks—creates long-term benefits, such as having calmer, more balanced responses to stressful situations.

These effects are directly related to the way our sense of smell affects emotional centers in the brain. As we saw earlier, certain scents can trigger long-buried memories, which generally have significant emotional resonance. Whether it's a positive or negative emotion depends on the memory, rather than on the scent.

27

For example, while stale cigar smoke might fall into the category of unpleasant scents for most people, if the smell of it reminds you of your grandfather, then interacting with that particular scent can be a very pleasant experience. Likewise, the scent of lilacs that others find pleasing might trigger in you a memory of a stressful environment where you used to work, or a past romantic relationship that ended in heartbreak. So while we can often agree on which scents are enjoyable and which are repulsive, we all have individual preferences based on our own experiences and our own unique sense of smell.

As our understanding of human biology has evolved, researchers have come to understand more about how our brains interact with olfactory stimuli. They have been able to trace a sort of "aromatic pathway" through the brain.

Once a scent is inhaled, it is processed by the olfactory system, which is connected to the limbic system which houses both memory and emotion. It is here that the emotional response to the scent is triggered. It's interesting to note that although the memory and emotion are interconnected, the memory itself doesn't have to be consciously recalled in order for an emotional response to occur—the scent reaches our emotional center with or without our ability to make a logical connection to it.

Of course, Witches and other magical practitioners never needed modern science to tell them that scent

28

has incredible power. In fact, we know that the implications for this power are far greater than mainstream science would imagine, because we have harnessed it to intentionally bring about changes we desire in our lives.

Whether those changes are related to material abundance, physical well-being, relationships or spiritual advancement, we are always using the same Universal energies to manifest our goals. And no matter what form of magic we're employing—candle spells, herb-and-crystal charms, ritual dance, etc.—we're always enacting the same basic magical equation: combining our personal power with Universal power to bring our desires into being.

THE MAGICAL POWER OF FOCUS

Magical botanical oils facilitate this process in two ways. The first is their direct effect on the mind of the magician. If scents can be used to elicit specific emotions and create a desired state of mind, then oils can be chosen according to their ability to bring about a conducive mental "platform" from which to perform magic.

For some people, the desired state of mind might differ according to the magical goal. For example, spellwork for peace and harmony in some aspect of your life might benefit from calming scents like lavender or vetiver, while livelier oils like bergamot and patchouli might be better suited for workings for prosperity.

Others take a different approach, having an oil or a blend of oils that consistently puts them in a particular "head space" from which they work all magic, no matter what the goal. Either way, the scent of the oil is contributing to the focused state of intention required for the work to be successful.

And make no mistake, focused intention *is* required for successful magic. Our ability to visualize our goal, to summon the emotions we anticipate feeling once the goal is achieved, and to channel this mental energy into the magical work is the personal power that we bring to the equation. Without this focus, we can't hook up with the Universal energies that make the change happen.

Imagine trying to turn on a lamp that isn't plugged into an electrical socket. Our focus is like the metal prongs of the plug—if we're not fully connected to the current of energy running through the socket, the light isn't going to come on.

Used properly, scented oils can help guide our focus so that we connect to Universal energies with perfect alignment, allowing our magical intention to flow out from us on the current of our personal power, and allowing the Universe to manifest it and send it back to us in realized form.

Again, this is the basic equation, or "formula," for all magic: personal power combined with Universal power creates change according to the intentions sent forth. Whether you're working with oils, herbs, candles, poppets, chanting and song, or simply with visualization, it always boils down to a matter of energy.

There is an infinite wealth of possibilities within this basic framework, with a broad range of tools and forms. As you practice and gain experience, you will likely find that some tools and forms of magic are easier or feel more natural to work with than others. Each of us has our own style and preferences and our own unique energy, so what works well for one person will not automatically work for another. But all tools of magic have magical potential if they're sufficiently charged with our focused, personal power.

NATURE'S POWER

That being said, there's actually an *extra* power inherent in some magical tools. Spell ingredients that physically embody the elements of Nature—crystals and stones, feathers and water, and even light, in the form of the color spectrum, carry within them their own magical energies, or their own unique manifestations of Universal energy.

These energies are often called magical properties, particularly when it comes to colors, crystals and herbs, but some magical traditions also assign specific properties to particular types of flowers, sea shells, and other natural items. These tools of Nature lend their energy to the magician's power—for we ourselves are also unique manifestations of Universal energy. With this extra power "boost" added to our own, we send our focused intention out into the Universe.

In the case of botanical oils, the boost of power comes from the energies of the trees, shrubs, flowers and other plants that are transformed into liquid form. Plants themselves are living beings, with their own living intelligence that works in perfect harmony with nature.

Plants actually embody all four physical elements, via soil, sunlight, rain and oxygen, and they participate in a growth cycle that is interdependent with the rest of their environment. They are also our allies in maintaining our own well-being, whether it's through balanced nutrition, the healing of injuries, or other forms of medicine, including methods that address emotional and spiritual well-being. For example, chamomile tea can calm inner turbulence, and simply sitting against the trunk of a tree can be grounding as well as uplifting.

And of course, plants have magical properties as well, which are highly concentrated in the form of essential oils. Indeed, the development of essential oils is in a sense a form of alchemy, whether or not this is recognized by most oil suppliers!

INCORPORATING OILS INTO YOUR PRACTICE

So how can you take your newfound understanding of the role of oils in magic and incorporate it into your practice? As with any aspect of magic, the key word is *practice*.

Having an intellectual grasp of the logic of magic is one thing, but it doesn't become real for any of us until we try it out on our own. If you're brand new to oils, it may be daunting to make choices about which one(s) to start experimenting with. But keeping the above discussion in mind, you might take one or more of the following approaches.

Your first option is to prioritize state of mind. This means choosing oils with scents that truly please you and aid your ability to focus calmly on the work at hand.

The actual spellwork you perform may or may not directly involve a specific oil, but you may want to anoint yourself with your favorite scent, or place a few drops in a diffuser to enhance your environment while you work. Plus, if you enjoy the scent of an oil, you're more likely to keep wanting to work with it, and repeated practice will only strengthen your magical skills.

The second option, which is a bit more traditional in terms of Western magic, is to choose oils according to their specific magical correspondences. If your spellwork is related to love, then rose, palmarosa, and/or other floral scents might be your best bet. If you're seeking to banish negative energy, then you'll probably want to choose cedarwood or sage. This approach is a bit more logical when it comes to using oils directly in your spellwork.

However, these two approaches are not mutually exclusive. As you experiment with different oils, you're bound to discover scents that are pleasing and beneficial to your state of mind, as well as having appropriate corresponding properties for your goal.

Furthermore, if you allow your intuition to guide you, you may just find that certain oils are calling to you, as herbs and crystals often do. This can happen when you're out shopping for oils and able to try them out from tester bottles, but also when you're simply reading the labels on the bottles. Or you may read about specific oils, as you will in Part Two, and get that certain feeling about one, a few, or even several of the oils discussed there.

NEXT STEPS

Now that you're well-versed in the origins and magical implications of botanical oils, it's time to start digging into the practical elements of oil magic. In Part Two, we'll cover basic tips on purchasing and storing essential oils.

You'll also be introduced to a Witch's dozen of single oils to consider for your own practice, with information about their healing and magical uses and suggestions for incorporating them into your spellwork.

This sets you up nicely for Part Three, where you'll find blending instructions, recipes, spells, and other ideas for making the most of the power of these magical botanical substances. You're already well on your way, so read on!

PART TWO

BUYING AND BLENDING MAGICAL OILS

PUTTING THE "CRAFT" IN WITCHCRAFT

One of the reasons many people are drawn to magic and Witchcraft is the element of hands-on creative activity. We don't just cast circles and stand inside them chanting magic words, or spend all day sitting at an altar while visualizing desired outcomes. Although all of these activities are useful and important, Witchcraft is about much more than ritual and ceremony.

Since ancient times, wise women and men have worked directly with the resources of Nature to make magical creations like charms, amulets, potions and brews. And some of the most powerful spellwork practiced today involves putting root powders, honey, stones and other ingredients into jars and bottles, sewing dried herbs into sachets and poppets, brewing special teas, and even baking magical treats!

There's so much opportunity to be creative in the world of the Craft that beginning Witches can often find themselves a bit overwhelmed. But there's nothing wrong with starting small—in fact, if you want to build a solid practice, it's a good idea to just choose one magical project to focus on at a time, until you get a feel for what you like to create and use in your magic.

Blending your own magical oils is a great place to start. It's a relatively simple process, and the finished work can be used multiple times in many different spells and rituals, so it's also quite an efficient use of your magical energy and time!

Of course, you can find plenty of pre-blended magical oils from reputable manufacturers, and these are perfectly fine to use in your spellwork. You may even want to try one or more store-bought blends as you're just starting out, to get an idea of which oils you like to work with. But creating your own blends puts you directly in touch with a magical tradition dating back thousands of years, helps you ensure that only natural, botanical ingredients are being used, and adds enormous personal power to your magic.

To create the highest quality blends, you'll need to know what to look for when purchasing your oils, and how to properly care for them, which we will cover below. Of course, you'll also need to get acquainted with each of your single oils on its own terms—its unique scent, its magical properties, and which oils to mix it with for a pleasing and powerful blend.

To get you off to a great start in this ancient art, you'll meet thirteen of the most popular essential oils used in Witchcraft today. So let's begin!

TIPS FOR PURCHASING BOTANICAL OILS

It should be noted that there's something of a limit to just how "DIY" you can be about creating your own magical blends. Some Witches want to take a completely "from-scratch" approach and make their own essential oils. However, this is almost never a feasible option.

Unless you have your own oil still, and access to vast quantities of the plants you want to extract essential oil from—not to mention plenty of patience and attention to detail—you're much better off purchasing essential oils from manufacturers who have already invested in the necessary equipment and know-how. It's far less expensive and time-consuming, and all but guarantees you the results you're looking for.

So even if you have a green thumb and a garden chock-full of herbs, put those plants to other magical uses, rather than risking them on a chemistry experiment that's unlikely to succeed!

You can still create unique and powerful "DIY" blends by using various single essential oils in combination. And you can also add your own special ingredients—like crystal shavings, flowers, and even herbs from that lush garden of yours—as we will see, below. First, though, let's consider some pointers for purchasing oils, and then get acquainted with a "Witch's dozen" of botanical oils widely used in ritual and magic.

THE CASE AGAINST SYNTHETICS

As we saw in Part 1, before the middle of the 19th century, scented oils and perfumes were made from all natural ingredients, and were considered rather precious commodities. Once synthetic fragrances were developed, however, it didn't take long for these imitation scents to be made widely available and often less expensive than their natural counterparts.

Over the last several decades, oils made with synthetic fragrances have come into widespread use in Wiccan and other Pagan religious and magical practices. Many Witches find it easier and more affordable to opt for synthetic versions of more expensive oils like rose, jasmine, and neroli.

However, the lack of natural ingredients in these oils makes them far inferior to true essential oils when it comes to magic. After all, it is the energetic properties of the plants, trees and flowers that essential oils are made from that pack the magical punch you're aiming for in your spellwork. By contrast, synthetic oils contain man-made chemicals, some of which can even be hazardous to your health.

It's true that scent of any kind can have a powerful effect on our personal energy and the energy of our environments. But it's the physical, natural, magical ingredients of essential oils that truly contribute to the manifestations we're setting in motion.

Just a few decades ago, essential oils were also relatively hard to obtain. Unless you lived in an area with a natural foods store or New Age shop, your only option was to send away for oils through the mail. However, due to the explosion of interest in aromatherapy which is spreading into even mainstream culture, and the advent of the internet, essential oils are far more widely available. And if you shop for them in person, you can often open a tester bottle, to see how you like the scent before you buy.

This ease of availability is another reason to choose these natural oils over their synthetic counterparts. As a Witch living in the 21st century, you owe it to yourself to use the gifts the Universe has offered you!

Of course, it's ultimately up to you to decide what to use in your magic. If you feel confident that synthetic oils will work for you, and you find yourself energetically attuning with them, no one is going to try to stop you! But this guide takes the philosophical standpoint that essential oils are actually an extension of herbal magic, and therefore the spellwork and other practical information throughout the guide assumes you are using true, natural ingredients.

BLENDING ON A BUDGET

Some popular magical essential oils are indeed quite expensive. This is due to various factors, including the complexity of the process, the availability of the raw plant materials, and the sheer amount of raw materials necessary to produce a significant quantity of oil. For example, 7.5 million jasmine flowers are required to make just 1 kilogram (35 oz) of essential oil. In fact, the most expensive oils tend to be florals, since delicate flower petals are difficult to process.

However, there are still plenty of options for budget-conscious Witches wanting to build up a decent collection of oils. Most citrus oils can be found for under $10, and many other magically useful oils fall between $10 and $20. Keep in mind that one bottle of oil can last up to a few years, as you're only using a very small amount at a time. So while there may be significant up-front costs, the overall investment in essentials is well worth it.

As for the more expensive "must-haves" like rose oil or jasmine, there are a couple of alternatives to consider: blends and absolutes. Sandalwood oil might be found in a love blend, for example, which can be significantly less expensive than sandalwood all by itself.

Of course, it's ideal to make your own magical blends, but you can find high-quality pre-blended oils through many Wiccan and other New Age retailers. Even blends designed chiefly for aromatherapy can be put to magical use with the appropriate intention and proper charging ritual.

If you prefer your expensive florals as single ingredients, many manufacturers sell "absolute" forms of rose, jasmine, and other florals containing a very small amount of the oil diluted in a carrier oil such as jojoba or coconut. These are not technically considered "essential oils" due to differences in the extraction process, which does involve chemical solvents. For this reason, absolutes are not recommended for medicinal use or even many aromatherapeutic uses. For magical purposes, however, there's no reason not to opt for these more affordable versions.

AVOIDING FAKES

As interest in aromatherapy and other uses for essential oils continues to grow, more and more new manufacturers are cropping up, both online and in retail stores. But while the variety of options to choose from is good news, there's also an increased likelihood of opportunistic, unethical vendors looking to make an easy buck.

Be careful and pay close attention when shopping for oils, or you could end up being fooled by false labeling. Just as the word "natural" often appears on packaged junk food that is anything but good for you, the word "essential" can be on a bottle of oil that actually contains synthetic fragrance. (That being said, do make sure that "essential" does appear on any oils you buy, or you can be sure that it is *not* essential oil.)

Unfortunately, there's often no actual way to tell whether a bottle of oil contains what it says it does until you've purchased it—and even then, it may not be obvious. For example, lavender oil is reported to be widely "adulterated," meaning that components are added to smell like lavender, in order to avoid having to use as much raw plant material to create the oil. Even experienced aromatherapists may have trouble telling the difference.

However, there are a few things you can look for that will help ensure you're not buying outright fakes.

Firstly, take note of the brand of the oil. Do some research online to look for positive (or negative) reviews and get a sense for the brand's popularity. This is especially important if you're buying online rather than in a store! If you're in a health food store, it's usually safe to assume that you're dealing with decent oil manufacturers, but oils found in "big box" store or other businesses that don't specifically cater to the organic-foods-and-alternative-medicine population may not be so trustworthy.

Secondly, consider the cost—if the price on the tag seems too good to be true, it's almost certainly not true essential oil. This can be a bit hard to gauge at first, since some are truly inexpensive, such as most citrus oils, while others like jasmine and neroli are out of most people's price ranges altogether. It's a good idea to shop around online and get a sense for average prices before purchasing an oil with an attractive price tag.

Another important thing to consider is the container the oil comes in. It should always be made of blue or brown glass—anything in plastic should be avoided no matter what!

Ideally, there should be a clear, round plug at the top of the bottle once the cap is unscrewed—this is an "orifice reducer" (also called a single-drop dispenser) that helps you control the amount of oil that comes out of the bottle. You may not be able to check for this before purchasing, but tester bottles in a store should have them, and online merchants are learning to show images of their uncapped oil bottles as well.

Finally, be sure that the plant's Latin name appears on the label. For example, a bottle of rosemary essential oil should have "rosmarinus officinalis" printed somewhere on it. Anything without the Latin name is likely to be a hybrid of various substances, possibly including synthetics, that add up to smell like rosemary.

STORING ESSENTIAL OILS

Many people new to essential oils make the mistake of thinking they can be stored anywhere in the home. This may be true if you use them enough to go through a bottle within a month or so, but if you want your oils to retain their proper scent and potency for long enough to make them worth their purchase price, be sure to keep them in a cool dark place.

If you're making your own blends, it's best to keep them in amber or cobalt glass bottles, rather than clear glass which lets in more light. (Do not use plastic bottles—the plastic will deteriorate.) Also, don't use glass droppers as lids for your bottles, no matter how handy it seems—the rubber tops will break down quickly, exposing the oils to oxygen and moisture and making a sticky mess!

Stored properly, essential oils can last up to five years or more, depending on the plant material they're made from. But because the compounds that make up essential oils are volatile, they don't retain their composition the way true, stable oils such as olive or coconut do.

"Volatile" doesn't mean that they will explode, although they are highly flammable, but that they vaporize quickly, and are easily affected by heat. If you leave them in a room where temperatures tend to fluctuate significantly, or in a place that gets direct sunlight, they will go "off" within a much shorter period of time. You may not be able to tell right away, but eventually you'll notice that the scent emitted from the bottle just doesn't smell as fresh and potent as it once did.

If you really want to be sure you're preserving the highest possible qualities in your oils, you can store them in the refrigerator, which many aromatherapists recommend. They're fine in the cold and will warm up quickly when held in your hand for a minute or two. (If you buy particularly high-grade oils and store them in the fridge, you may want to keep them in a ziplock bag, as their scent can be transferred to some foods.)

Another important aspect of volatility is oxidation—when essential oil is exposed to oxygen consistently, the oil will evaporate more quickly and the quality will deteriorate. (This is good to keep in mind if you're sampling tester oils in a shop—if they've been opened a lot, they won't smell exactly like the oil in the sealed bottle you're purchasing.)

Of course, this eventually happens to all oils over time, but you can certainly keep the process very gradual with proper care. Be sure your bottles are tightly capped, and don't leave them open for longer than necessary. Some people recommend transferring oils to a smaller bottle once they're approaching empty, to avoid having too much oxygen interacting with the remaining oil.

The more "high-maintenance" approaches described above, such as refrigerator storage and transference to smaller bottles are recommended by aromatherapists and others who use essential oils for healing as opposed to (or in addition to) magic.

Depending on your intentions, you may not need to take such stringent precautions. Especially if you don't use oils for anything other than anointing candles or other magical tools, it doesn't strictly matter if the scent is a bit less fresh than it was when you bought and/or blended your oils.

However, if you're going to invest in true botanical oils, you may as well store them properly in case you get a hankering to try them in the bath or heat them in an oil burner or diffuser at some point!

THIRTEEN
MAGICAL OILS

The oils included in this guide were selected according to several criteria. First and foremost, they are among the most popular ingredients in ritual and spellwork among contemporary Witches. Most also have a history of magical use dating back at least several centuries, if not further.

The descriptions below include the chief magical uses for each oil and a few suggestions for incorporating them into your practice. You'll also find magical correspondences for each—Elemental, planetary, zodiac and even deity associations, for those who honor and/or work with specific deities in their magical practice.

These oils were also selected with affordability in mind, to make it easier for you to choose essential oils over synthetics. Some, like lemon and clove, can easily be found for under $10, while most hover in the $10 to $20 range.

Several powerful and delightful oils, such as jasmine, sandalwood and neroli, have been omitted due to their potentially prohibitive costs. The only exception to the price range limit is rose oil, which tends to start at around $50. It is included here because it's widely considered a must-have by Witches, especially when it comes to spellwork related to love. (Again, for those who can't afford true essential rose oil, blends or absolute dilutions are a possible option.)

Other considerations included a diverse range of magical properties and a balanced selection of scent categories—floral, citrus, spicy, earthy, and so on. Every oil on the list can be used for at least two or three different magical purposes, and can be blended with at least one, if not several of the others on the list. So even if you start with just two or three oils, you can begin experimenting with creating your own blends.

Finally, each oil has useful aromatherapeutic benefits, for those interested in exploring them. After all, if you're going to purchase essential oils, you may as well get the most value for your money! In fact, many Witches don't see a hard and fast distinction between using oils for aromatherapy and using them in ritual and spellwork. Particularly for those inclined toward "green" witchery, oil magic is a fairly common aspect of everyday life!

It's important to note a few safety precautions here. First, the medicinal information provided for each oil is *for informational purposes only.* You will see that no specific directions are given for medical use of essential oils—for this, you would need to consult an aromatherapist or other professional healer.

Second, although some essential oils are considered safe for internal use, there is a lot of debate about whether it's really a good idea to ingest these volatile substances. Particularly if you're going for the least expensive brands, which are likely to be of a lower quality, it's best to avoid using oils internally. There are no instructions for internal use within this guide, but given the wide range of information found online regarding essential oils, it's worth cautioning those who are new to oils and may be tempted to experiment.

Finally, pregnant women are advised to use extra caution when dealing with essential oils, even for topical use or simply inhaling the scents. This is particularly the case during the first trimester. Several of the 13 described below have been cited as oils to avoid throughout pregnancy. Others may not be recommended during nursing.

Obviously, research and check with your physician before using any essential oils if you are pregnant or nursing. In addition, people with medical conditions like diabetes or asthma should check with their physicians before interacting with essential oils.

Remember that you don't have to go out and buy a bunch of essential oils tomorrow in order to get started with oil magic. In fact, it can be nicer to begin with just one or two, getting to know each one individually before adding more to your stock. Three is a nice magical number, and is ideal for learning to make your own blends, but always go with what you can afford. After all, if you're stressed about the expense of buying them, that energy will come through in your spellwork, which rather defeats the purpose of using them in the first place!

So how do you choose which oil(s) to purchase first? As you read through these descriptions, pay attention to your intuition. Most likely, some oils will stand out to you more than others. The ones that pique your interest the most are helping you to determine where to begin. After you've gotten comfortable working with a small selection of oils, you can gradually bring in additional oils that blend well with what you already have in your growing collection!

BERGAMOT
(CITRUS BERGAMIA)

Bergamot is the fruit of a citrus tree, which is related to the orange tree, but far more bitter and not generally eaten on its own. It takes its name from the Italian province of Bergamo, where it was first cultivated after being brought to Europe from its native Morocco (it is also native to many parts of Asia).

For centuries, it was used in Italian folk medicine, but remained largely unknown to the rest of the Western world until more recent times. Tea drinkers may recognize its floral, citrus scent as part of the unique flavor of Earl Grey tea, which is made with bergamot oil. It is also used in many classic fragrance blends. The essential oil is derived from the peel of the fruit.

Once used primarily for treating fevers, bergamot's antiseptic properties have been applied in modern times to combat infections—particularly in the lungs and urinary tract. Its interesting combination of uplifting and calming energies make it effective for a variety of physical ailments, including insect bites and other skin injuries, as well as ulcers, colds and flu, and even tonsillitis.

On the emotional and spiritual levels, bergamot essential oil is great for relieving stress, grief, and depression, and enhancing joy and strength. Inhaling the scent of bergamot is uplifting to the inner self and can promote restful sleep—which is key to maintaining an overall balance of mind, body, and spirit!

Magically, bergamot is strongly associated with the Sun, and is used in rituals to clear the mind and spirit, dispelling the shadows of depression, despondency, and fogginess that can come from focusing too much on worry and problems. It can help us reconnect to our higher selves, lightening us up so that we can once again enjoy humor and happiness.

It also has a protective quality, shielding us from negative impulses that may be lurking in the shadows of our thought patterns. If you feel a slide into sadness or despair coming on, use a few drops of bergamot oil in a ritual bath to sort yourself out!

Bergamot also has a strong association with prosperity, and is used in plenty of magic related to success. Its energies can be directed to helping you spend your money wisely, and being on the alert for new opportunities to bring more into your life. Place three drops of the oil on your purse or wallet to attract cash, or use it in a sachet to bring success in all your endeavors.

Other magical associations for bergamot include peace, confidence, and harmony. Use it to help you resolve conflicts in a way that keeps your self-worth intact without inflicting harm on others.

Note: Bergamot is a photosensitizing oil, meaning that it can cause severe burns if worn on the skin during exposure to the Sun. Several citrus oils fall into this category, but bergamot poses a substantially higher risk than any other.

If you're wanting to wear an oil blend that includes bergamot, either stay out of direct sunlight altogether, or use a bergaptene-free bergamot oil, which is re-distilled to remove the component that causes photosensitivity. It should also not be used by pregnant women.

Bergamot blends well with other citrus oils like lemon, neroli, orange, geranium and lemon verbena, as well as lavender, cinnamon, rose, clary sage and jasmine.

Magical Associations:

Element: Fire, Air
Planet: Sun, Mercury
Zodiac: Gemini, Virgo
Deities: Persephone, Fortuna, Hermes, Mercury

CEDARWOOD
(CEDRUS ATLANTICA)

There are many different species of cedar trees found around the world, but the source of the original essential oil known as cedarwood is the Atlas cedar, a native tree of the Atlas mountains in North Africa.

This tree was highly valued by the ancient Egyptians, who believed it to be imperishable and therefore used the oil to anoint and embalm the bodies of their dead, and made coffins from the wood. Cedarwood was also used for incense and cosmetics.

Other sources of cedar oil were found in different parts of the globe, including Celtic Europe, where it was used to preserve the heads of enemies killed in battle, and North America, where indigenous cultures have long been using cedar for purification and protection.

When shopping for cedarwood oil, you may find other Latin names such as *juniperus virginiana,* denoting a different but related species of tree. If this is the case, don't be too concerned about it—the magical properties of cedar oil are essentially the same, regardless of the source.

Distilled from the wood and bark, as opposed to from the foliage (which is known as cedar leaf oil), cedarwood oil is used in alternative medicine for healing inflammatory conditions like bronchitis, arthritis, and acne. At the emotional level, its aromatherapeutic properties are good for calming and centering, finding balance and releasing fear, anger and aggression.

Spiritually, cedarwood oil can be used to purify the energies of your home when heated in an oil burner, a diffuser or a simmering pot of water. Some people like to inhale the woody, clean, sweet aroma before taking part in rituals to enhance their connection to divine energies.

Cedarwood is used in magical workings related to self-control, healing, and strengthening one's spirituality. It has traditionally been relied on by people who believe themselves to be "hexed," so its energetic properties are good for halting and reversing a "spell of bad luck," regardless of what the suspected cause may be. Try using it in satchels for protection or healing. Spellwork related to banishing and releasing also goes will with cedarwood, as do spells for attracting power, pride, and strength.

Some traditions consider it to be a good attractor of prosperity and wealth, so it's a good one to add to a money spell in conjunction with other ingredients with these associations. However, its core properties are related more to rebirth and regeneration, which happens only after we release what no longer serves us, so if you're using cedarwood oil for prosperity, try it in the context of removing obstacles to your financial well-being. Spells and rituals related to balance and steadiness and the fortitude to stay on your spiritual path are also in alignment with the properties of this oil.

Cedarwood blends well with its relative, juniper oil, as well as bergamot, neroli, clary sage, rosemary, vetiver, ylang ylang, and other floral scents. It's best to avoid using cedarwood during pregnancy.

Magical Associations:

Element: Fire
Planet: Sun
Zodiac: Aries, Sagittarius
Deities: Pan, Aphrodite, Cernunnos, Artemis, Isis, Jupiter

CINNAMON
(CINNAMOMUM ZEYLANICUM)

Most people who use cinnamon sticks or ground cinnamon in their cooking are actually using cassia (*cinnamomum cassia*), a close relative of "true cinnamon" (*cinnamomum zeylanicum*), with a similar flavor and aroma, but more widely available and therefore less expensive.

Essential oil of cinnamon theoretically comes from the "true" tree, but since most people can't detect the difference, many oil manufacturers may blend the two together. The inner bark of the tree is what most cinnamon oil is distilled from—especially if the bottle specifies "cinnamon bark. However, oil is also distilled from the leaves.

Companies that sell both leaf and bark oils will usually label them accordingly, but there are some manufacturers who combine the two. Unless you're using these oils for a specific medical purpose, the differences are not significant, so there's no need to sweat over the degree of "purity" of this essential oil. Just know that the less you pay for it, the less likely it is that you're getting unadulterated true cinnamon bark oil.

Like cedarwood, cinnamon oil was included in ancient Egyptian embalming potions, as well as incense and perfumes. As a spice, cinnamon was prized throughout the ancient world, and the herb was also part of magic and ritual.

Today, cinnamon essential oil is used in treatments for intestinal problems and other stress-related issues. Its aromatherapeutic properties make it a warming, reviving, and uplifting oil. Many people find it to have aphrodisiac qualities, as well as an overall booster of physical strength and energy.

Inhaling the scent can help you focus on strengthening your physical body as well as opening up to psychic receptivity. Be sure to go easy on the inhalation, though—this is a "hot" oil that can irritate your nose, so use a diffuser, or waft the scent toward you with your hand rather than breathing it straight up your nose!

Key magical properties of cinnamon oil include protection, prosperity, psychic awareness, and love. Spellwork related to all of these goals, as well as physical energy and healing, is appropriate for this oil. Anoint a dollar bill with cinnamon and keep it in your wallet to attract money. Do some visualization work around protection or health while breathing in the scent from the bottle or from a diffuser.

Use a drop or two in a love blend and anoint a candle with it to spice up a relationship. If you're feeling down or lonely, call on the assistance of cinnamon to transmute those negative feelings with its fiery power. If you have good food grade cinnamon oil, place one drop of it in a tea to fire up your psychic receptivity.

Take note: cinnamon oil is a skin irritant, so be extra careful when handling the undiluted oil, and never use it in bathwater or any blends you plan to wear on your skin. Avoid using during pregnancy.

Cinnamon's warm, sweet, spicy aroma blends well with other spicy oils like clove, nutmeg, and black pepper, citrus oils like bergamot and lemon, as well as rose, chamomile, frankincense, ginger, and rosemary.

Element: Fire
Planet: Sun
Zodiac: Aries, Leo
Deities: Aphrodite/Venus, Demeter, Mercury, Bast, Ra, Brighid

CLOVE
(EUGENIA CARYOPHYLLATA)

What we know as cloves are actually flower buds from a tropical evergreen tree, which are harvested before the flowers open, sun dried, and then sold either whole or ground for culinary use.

Clove essential oil is distilled from the buds and, usually, the leaves of the tree—although some manufacturers specify their oil as "clove bud." The clove tree originated in Indonesia, where it was traditionally considered sacred, but cloves were popular in ancient Egypt, Greece, Rome, and China.

Medicinally, clove oil is probably best known for its ability to calm down a toothache (though this should only be used until you can get to your dentist to take care of the underlying cause). It is also used to prevent and relieve indigestion. Its aromatherapeutic properties are similar to those of cinnamon, but clove oil's indications include asthma and bronchitis in addition to digestive and stress-related problems.

On the cognitive and emotional levels, clove oil promotes courage, memory retrieval, and the awakening of the senses. It promotes healing on all levels, but particularly the release of fears related to the past that keep us stuck, helping us to move forward.

Use clove oil in magic related to courage, protection and purification—particularly of the home or other spaces where you spend a lot of time. This can be achieved with a drop or two in an oil burner, a diffuser or even in mopping solution, if you have tile or hardwood floors.

Clove drives away negativity, so it can also be used in banishing and releasing spells of all kinds. Use it to repel negative thoughts about yourself or others, and to ward off gossip.

It also draws wisdom and inspiration to start anew in relation to any long-standing goal or project. This is related to its ability to dispel fear, so if you have been putting off a dream due to fear of failure (or fear of success!), clove is a good oil to help you turn this situation around.

As with cinnamon, wealth is another association for clove, due to its warming and stimulating properties.

Use it as a "booster" to prosperity spells and money blends.

Some wear clove oil on the body to attract love, but this isn't ideal for everyone, since it can be irritating to the skin. As with cinnamon oil, use caution when handling it undiluted, and use it very sparingly in blends intended for use on the skin. Some people are more sensitive to clove than others, so you might want to do a small test patch before using it in any body blends. Avoid use during pregnancy.

Clove has a very distinct robust, sweet yet earthy smell that blends well with other spicy oils like cinnamon and nutmeg, citrus oils like lemon, orange, and bergamot, as well as lavender, rosemary, peppermint, clary sage and ylang ylang.

Magical Associations:

Element: Fire
Planet: Jupiter
Zodiac: Pisces, Scorpio, Sagittarius
Deities: Osiris, Isis, Toth

JUNIPER
(JUNIPERUS COMMUNIS)

Juniper is the name of a variety of coniferous plants, ranging from shrubs to tall trees. Juniper has been called a sacred tree of the Druids, and was used in several religious rites and traditions of the Celtic Isles, including the Beltane fires. The small cones produced by *juniperus communis* ("common juniper") resemble berries and are used to flavor gin and some northern European dishes.

The oil is made by distilling the needles, wood and berries of the plant, but oil is also made with the berries alone. Juniper berry oil is considered far superior to regular juniper oil when it comes to medicinal uses, but regular juniper oil still has many aromatherapeutic benefits. For magical purposes, both oils will work equally well.

The purifying and clearing properties of juniper make it particularly useful for skin conditions such as acne and eczema. It also helps regulate appetite and detoxify the body, heal infections, and resolve anxiety. As an aromatherapeutic agent, juniper oil has a purifying and uplifting effect when inhaled or added to a diffuser or oil burner. It aids in positive thinking and coming back into balance with regard to diet and exercise.

On the spiritual level, this scent helps clear the way for a stronger connection with our inner selves, removing mental and emotional blocks to the truths we seek. Burning or diffusing juniper during meditation can facilitate powerfully enlightening experiences that help us understand the root causes of negative feelings.

Purification and protection are the main magical uses for juniper oil, whether you're dealing with people or environments. For self-protection, visualize a white-green glowing light around you, guarding you from negative energies as you inhale the fresh, evergreen scent. Try wearing 2 or 3 drops as an added protection against illness and accidents.

For safeguarding your home, add a few drops to water used for mopping floors and dusting, and/or wash the outside of doors, windows, and other potential entry points where unwanted energy might drift in. You can also keep the oil in a diffuser near each door. Any spellwork related to purification, protection, or healing will benefit from a juniper-anointed candle. Use it in any oil blends related to these purposes as well.

Some find juniper oil to have an aphrodisiac quality and may wear it, use it in a sachet, or add it to a magical bath to attract love. Although other oils like cinnamon or rose would seem to be much more appropriate for love magic, those who find themselves consistently drawn into negative or abusive relationships may want to try juniper's energies instead, as its purifying and protective properties can help clear out old patterns and make way for healthier ones.

Juniper oil is particularly susceptible to evaporation, so be sure you keep your bottle tightly capped, away from sources of heat, and stored in a cool, dark place. Avoid using during pregnancy.

Juniper blends well with other evergreens like cedarwood and cypress, citrus oils like lemon, grapefruit and bergamot, as well as lavender, geranium, and vetiver.

Magical Associations:

Element: Fire
Planet: Sun, Jupiter
Zodiac: Aries, Leo, Sagittarius
Deities: Astarte, Ishtar, Pan, Brighid

LAVENDER
(LAVANDULA ANGUSTIFOLIA)

Lavender is an evergreen shrub with small aromatic purple or blue flowers, which are distilled to make the essential oil. It's native to the Mediterranean regions, but is now one of the most widely cultivated herbs in the Western Hemisphere.

Lavender was well known to the ancient Egyptians, Arabs, Greeks and Romans, who used it for everything from fragrance to medicine to mummification. In fact, the first essential oil distilleries were created in ancient Arabia in order to make lavender perfume. Today, many Witches and other

Pagans toss dried lavender into bonfires at Midsummer rituals to honor their deities.

Lavender's popularity throughout the ages can be linked not just to its calming effects and pleasant scent, but also its antiseptic and anti-inflammatory properties. Medicinally, it's one of the world's oldest antibacterial agents, used by the ancient Romans to fumigate sick rooms, and used today to soothe throat infections, insect bites, intestinal upset, inflammation and more. In aromatherapy, lavender oil is particularly prized for its ability to promote restful sleep, relieve tension and headaches, and ease depression.

Lavender's healing successes often provide a clear window onto the mind-body connection, as its relaxing effects on the mind lead to improved symptoms in the physical body. It is said that regular inhalation of lavender scent promotes longevity.

In the emotional and spiritual realms, lavender oil promotes a sense of serenity and well-being. Its scent is steadying to the psyche, helping us to feel protected and cared for and to resolve emotional conflicts.

One of the easiest ways to use lavender is to sprinkle a drop or two on your pillow at night for deeper sleep. Use it in bath blends for purification, relieving depression, emotional balance, and help with making a difficult decision. Keep a bottle nearby during difficult times, whether you're dealing with grief, stress, or uncertainty about an important situation.

Magically, lavender oil is used in workings related to health, peace, and banishing negative energy. It can also be incorporated into love spells (specifically, the scent is traditionally said to attract men) and used as part of a love blend, either to wear on the body or to anoint a charm. However, romantic love is not necessarily indicated for all uses of lavender—it is also said to be good for promoting love of a strictly platonic and/or spiritual nature, and even celibacy.

Some also use lavender for promoting financial wealth and business success. Add it to a money blend containing patchouli and/or other prosperity oils and anoint your wallet, purse, or change jar.

Newcomers to lavender oil should note that unlike the dried herb which has a fairly light and mild scent, the essential oil is very potent—so use it very sparingly until you get a sense of how much you can enjoy without getting overwhelmed.

Most lavender is considered safe for use in pregnancy after the first trimester, but avoid using *lavandula stoechas,* known also as French lavender or Spanish lavender.

The earthy, yet somewhat floral scent of lavender blends well with most oils, but particularly citrus oils like bergamot and lemon, evergreens like cedarwood and pine, and spicy oils like clove and black pepper. Rosemary, patchouli, chamomile, geranium, vetiver and even peppermint are also good companions for lavender.

Magical Associations:

Element: Air
Planet: Mercury
Zodiac: Gemini, Virgo, Aquarius
Deities: Demeter, Cernunnos, Hecate, Saturn, Bridhid

LEMON
(CITRUS LIMONUM)

The fruit we know today as the lemon is a descendant of an ancient, less juicy and more bitter fruit commonly referred to as citron. Originating in Southeast Asia, the citron eventually made its way around the ancient world, where it was used for a variety of purposes, including relieving digestive issues from food poisoning, killing insects, and as an ingredient in perfume.

The citron was a good luck charm in some cultures, and is believed to have been placed in Egyptian tombs along with other fruits to accompany the deceased into the afterlife. Today, it is an important part of rituals during the Jewish harvest holiday of

Sukkot, and is used in China as an offering in Buddhist temples.

It is possible to find citron essential oil today, but lemon oil is far more widely available and has the same basic properties. Like bergamot, lemon oil is extracted from the peel of the fruit, and has a refreshing, uplifting scent.

Its purifying and reviving properties are used to treat acne, poor circulation, colds, fever and infections, among other ailments. Some have found its energizing properties so potent that they inhale the scent first thing in the morning as an alternative to a cup of coffee!

Lemon oil is a great detoxifier of mind, body, and spirit, and can be used to clear away mental clutter and psychic debris left over from past emotional experiences.

In the realm of the Craft, lemon oil is associated with the Moon, making it a powerful addition to Full Moon rituals. A few drops in a cup of water makes an excellent purification solution for magical tools such as crystals, amulets, and other ritual objects. (Note: avoid using lemon oil on tools made from pewter.)

Using lemon oil in a burner or diffuser will clear the negativity from a room immediately, and open up your psyche for positive energy to enter. Spellwork related to healing is highly compatible with lemon oil—try anointing a yellow candle with lemon and visualize your vibrational frequency rising to the level of optimal health as the candle burns.

This scent is also great for resolving indecisiveness about a troubling or puzzling issue in your life. Burn or diffuse some lemon oil while meditating, and then use a pendulum to help you clarify your best next steps. Use lemon in oil blends related to purification, healing, longevity and spiritual awareness.

As a citrus oil, lemon is also photosensitizing. While it doesn't appear to carry the same level of risk as bergamot, it's still recommended to avoid exposure to direct sunlight if wearing a blend containing this oil.

Lemon's sharp, sweet, citrusy scent blends well with a variety of oils including other citruses like bergamot and neroli, evergreens like juniper and eucalyptus, and florals like rose, geranium ylang ylang, along with chamomile and frankincense.

Magical Associations:

Element: Water
Planet: Moon
Zodiac: Pisces, Cancer
Deities: Athena, Diana, Luna, Neptune

PALMAROSA
(CYMBOPOGON MARTINI)

While palmarosa may not be as well-known as other, more popular essential oils in use today, it is actually found in a wide variety of products, including food and beverages, soap, perfume and skin care products.

The oil is distilled from a perennial grass native to South Asia, and has been used for centuries for both cosmetic and medicinal purposes. The ancient healers of India treated fever, infections, rheumatism and nerve pain with palmarosa oil, and it was also an ingredient in Indian incense blends as well as an insect repellent.

Once it was introduced into Persia via trade, it began to catch on in the West as well, and due to its floral scent was often used as a substitute for, or additive to, rose oil, which was (and still is) far more expensive.

Palmarosa's healing attributes are chiefly used in skincare, as its antiseptic, calming properties promote cell stimulation and regulation. It can successfully treat acne, dermatitis and minor skin infections, and even reduce the visibility of scar tissue and wrinkles. In addition, palmarosa has been used for nervous exhaustion and digestive issues.

On the emotional level, this oil promotes an overall sense of well-being, banishing stress and depressive vibrations and encouraging joy and positive thoughts. Inhaling the scent can have a calming effect on the spirit, relieving the tension that leads to disconnection from one's inner self and promoting clear thinking and enthusiasm for meeting life's challenges.

Magically, palmarosa oil is used in spellwork and rituals related to healing, love, and loyalty—to both oneself and to others. It is particularly useful in workings aimed at healing a broken heart, and/or feelings of being neglected or misunderstood. If need be, it can be used as a substitute for rose oil in love spells, though it's best to combine it with geranium or another strong floral if using it for this purpose. However, it's a perfect love spell ingredient in its own right, and can be used in body oils, ritual baths, and sachets for attracting new love or strengthening existing relationships.

Like lemon oil, palmarosa is conducive to spellwork around physical healing, in conjunction with any required medical care. Use it as a visualizing aid during healing spells, focusing on both the physical and emotional conditions you desire.

Palmarosa is also particularly suited to assist with situations involving change, difficult transitions, and feelings of jealousy and insecurity. Write down your concerns on parchment or journaling paper, anoint it with the oil, and then burn the paper over a sink or other fire-proof basin. The calming and soothing properties of palmarosa also make it a good oil for burning or diffusing prior to magical rituals, in order to promote positive focus.

Palmarosa's sweet, floral, almost-lemony scent blends well with floral oils like geranium, rose and ylang ylang, and citrus oils like bergamot and lime, as well as sandalwood, cedarwood, and lemongrass.

Magical Associations:

Element: Water
Planet: Venus
Zodiac: Pisces, Cancer, Libra
Deities: Demeter, Athena

PATCHOULI
(POGOSTEMON CABLIN)

Another oil that can be traced far back in human history, patchouli has been part of Ayurvedic medicine for thousands of years and is part of traditional medicines of China, Japan and Malaysia.

Used in many cultures for practical purposes such as keeping moths away from clothing and warding off illness, the plant also has a a widespread reputation as an aphrodisiac and a long history of inclusion in seductive perfumes, love potions and magical charms.

A member of the mint family, patchouli has a very distinct scent which some people find unpleasant, while others are strongly drawn to it.

Patchouli essential oil is derived from the distillation of the leaves and flowers. There are a few varieties of the patchouli plant that are commercially available, including *pogostemon heyeanus* and *pogostemon patchouli*. The *cablin* species is considered the best for sourcing the essential oil, followed by the *patchouli*. The *heyeanus* variety is not very fragrant at all and makes a poor source for the oil, so avoid purchasing products with this name on it.

Medicinally, patchouli has anti-fungal properties, making it an effective aid in resolving dermatitis, dandruff, and chapped skin. It also has both stimulating and calming properties, depending on the amount used—smaller amounts act as a stimulant, while large doses have a sedative effect. This being said, the oil is more of a stimulant than a sedative, so although it can be very useful for grounding and centering, it is not recommended for promoting restful sleep.

On an emotional level, patchouli can help level out a high-strung state, bringing us back to Earth and facilitating a calm, reasonable approach to conflicts or problems. For this reason, it is also said to assist in reducing "emotional eating" habits.

Patchouli is a popular ingredient in body fragrances, as continual exposure to the scent helps keep the wearer grounded and feeling peaceful. However, on its own, patchouli is not particularly favored for use in oil burners or diffusers. Instead, try blending it with other compatible oils for a pleasant, calming atmosphere in your home or sacred space. Patchouli's spiritual properties are very useful for mediation, particularly when you've been feeling disconnected from your inner self.

Magically, the key goals of patchouli include love, lust, money, and physical energy. To attract money into your life, anoint a five or ten-dollar bill and keep it in your wallet, or add a drop or two to prosperity charms. A green candle anointed with patchouli is a key staple of money spells.

For increasing sexual desire, add patchouli to a bath and/or wear it as a fragrance on a date, but make sure you actually enjoy the scent before doing so, as it will not work if you don't find it pleasing. If you want to use it for love magic but find the scent overpowering, you can add it to a love sachet and keep it in your purse when going out.

For spells to increase physical energy, anoint and burn a red or orange candle. Patchouli is also used to repel negative energies.

Unlike most essential oils, patchouli actually gets better with age. The earthy, slightly sweet scent will become richer and deeper over time, provided it is stored properly.

Patchouli blends well with other earthy oils like rosemary and lavender, evergreens like cedarwood and juniper, and florals like rose, geranium and ylang ylang, along with vetiver, clary sage and sandalwood.

Magical Associations:

Element: Earth
Planet: Saturn
Zodiac: Taurus, Virgo, Capricorn, Aquarius
Deities: Hecate, Pan, Aphrodite, Hestia

PEPPERMINT
(MENTHA PIPERITA)

A hybrid cross between spearmint and watermint, the peppermint plant has a long history of culinary, medicinal, and spiritual uses going back to ancient Rome and beyond. It's among the most popular oils used in aromatherapy today, with a wide variety of applications, not least of which is a powerful repellant of ants and mice. The essential oil of peppermint is distilled from the leaves of the plant.

Peppermint's cooling, refreshing properties make it ideal for soothing stomach upsets including nausea and indigestion. Simply inhaling the scent of the essential oil can bring immediate relief. Peppermint also works well on headaches—try anointing your temples with a small drop of the oil to release cranial tension. For mild burns (including sunburn) and itchy skin, place a cloth soaked in water with a few drops over the affected area. Peppermint has also been used to reduce fever and soothe tired, achy joints.

On the mental level, peppermint oil is excellent for awakening the conscious mind and chasing away fogginess and lethargy. Along with lemon oil, it's a great one to have on hand for studying and other tasks that require concentration. On the emotional level, it can be used to clear away negativity and hopelessness, opening the space required for positive energy and joy.

Spiritually, peppermint's properties help facilitate optimism in the face of the unknown, helping us to accept life's mysteries and enjoy the unfolding of new developments, rather than reacting in fear.

In magic, peppermint oil can help to dissolve obstacles, and so is an excellent choice for spellwork around issues that have seemed unresolvable. Use it for situations where you need to get energy moving again in the right direction, whether it's related to finances, relationships, home environment, etc.

Peppermint is also a very pleasant purifier that raises the vibrations of any space it is used in. Try several drops in a cleaning solution for your floors, walls and furniture to cleanse all negativity from your home, place a few drops in a diffuser or oil burner, and/or use it directly on candles in purification rituals.

When it comes to wearing it in a body blend or adding it to a bath, use caution, and do a small patch test to see how well you tolerate it. Some people find the cooling properties too overpowering to be comfortable on the skin.

One interesting aspect of peppermint's dual qualities of reviving and cooling shows up in its use as a dreaming agent. Many find peppermint oil to be an excellent catalyst for positive dreams that shed light on issues in waking life, and will use peppermint in dream sachets under their pillow.

However, depending on your own body chemistry, peppermint may keep you awake rather than promoting restful sleep. You may need to experiment to find out how you respond to this unique essential oil. If it turns out that it keeps you up, you might use it in a "dreaming spell" early in the evening, and then turn to lavender or another calming oil before going to bed. Avoid using peppermint oil during pregnancy.

Peppermint's unique, minty scent makes it a little less agreeable with a wide variety of oils than the others featured in this guide. However, it can be blended in small amounts with lavender, eucalyptus, rosemary, geranium, lemon, and some spicy oils like cinnamon and clove. You may also discover other good combinations with peppermint as you experiment on your own.

Magical Associations:

Element: Earth, Air, Fire
Planet: Mercury, Mars
Zodiac: Aries, Gemini, Virgo, Aquarius
Deities: Artemis, Hecate, Cernunnos

ROSE
(ROSA SPP)

Arguably the world's most well-known flower of all time, and cultivated for at least 5,000 years, the rose is valued for far more than its romantic symbolism.

The ancient Egyptians grew roses in their temple gardens, and exported them throughout the civilizations of the Mediterranean region. Both rosewater and rose essential oil have been used for centuries in both cosmetic and medicinal applications.

The oil is often labelled as "rose otto" ("otto" meaning "essence") in order to distinguish it from rosewater, which is usually a by-product of the distillation process used to make the oil.

There are over one hundred natural species of rose, and thousands of cultivated varieties, but most essential oil is made from *rosa damascena*, which is grown mostly in Bulgaria, and *rosa centifolia*, which largely comes from North Africa. *Rosa gallica* is another source, which is grown mostly in Turkey and is considered by many people to be too heavy and overpowering compared to the other two varieties.

But no matter which source you're considering, expect the price to be quite high—between $50 and $125 for one ounce. Any oil costing considerably less is certainly adulterated, either with other, cheaper oils (such as palmarosa or geranium), synthetic ingredients, or both.

What makes rose oil so much more expensive than most other essentials is the cost of producing it—over two tons of rose petals are needed to make one pound of essential oil.

Furthermore, the petals can only be picked before sunrise, since the oil contained within the petals evaporates in the heat of the day, which puts limits on the rate of production. But if your budget simply doesn't have room for a bottle of pure rose oil, you can definitely make do with a blend or an absolute, as discussed above.

Rose oil is highly valued for its assistance in balancing hormones, which helps with menstrual issues and insomnia, as well as improving poor circulation and soothing stress-related conditions. Its comforting and uplifting properties help boost confidence, resolve domestic conflicts, and promote a general sense of peaceful well-being.

Considered a balm for the heart, rose is also traditionally considered an aphrodisiac scent, and can be used to restore loving feelings in a romantic relationship. Simply placing one or two drops in a diffuser or burner can dramatically improve the energy in your home, creating a loving atmosphere.

In fact, love magic tends to be the primary use for rose essential oil. Whether worn as a fragrance, added to a love sachet or ritual bath, or used on a red candle in a love spell, rose oil is a quintessential ingredient in spellwork aimed at attracting a lover or rejuvenating an existing relationship.

However, rose is also excellent for manifesting healing, balance, peace and general contentment with life, no matter your relationship status. It can also be used in spells and charms related to physical beauty, patience and protection.

Since the scent is quite powerful and the oil quite expensive, you might want to add just a drop or two to other oils in a blend, as opposed to using rose on its own the way you might use other less powerful, more affordable oils. However, like patchouli, rose oil improves with age, so don't worry about hanging on to the same bottle for years.

Its heady, floral scent blends well with other florals like geranium, ylang ylang and neroli, earthy scents like patchouli and sandalwood, and various other oils including bergamot, vetiver and black pepper.

Magical Associations:

Element: Earth, Water, Fire
Planet: Saturn, Venus
Zodiac: Taurus, Cancer, Libra, Sagittarius
Deities: Aphrodite/Venus, Demeter, Isis

VETIVER
(VETIVERA ZIZANIOIDES)

Known as "the oil of tranquility" in India and Sri Lanka where vetiver originated, this essential oil comes from a perennial grass that now grows in many tropical countries.

Vetiver is also known "magic grass," "miracle grass" and "wonder grass" in various parts of the world, due to its medicinal and magical properties as well as its usefulness in rehabilitating barren and polluted land. An aromatic plant, it has long been used in Southeast Asia to thatch huts and make blinds to keep out the intense heat. When water is sprinkled on the blinds, the aromatic properties are activated, emitting the refreshing scent of vetiver.

Unlike the other oils featured in this guide, the essential oil of vetiver is distilled solely from the root of the plant. The root has also been used in traditional folk magic to promote safety and increase abundance.

Vetiver's soothing, calming qualities make it useful for resolving nervous tension and insomnia, while its grounding and uplifting properties can assist with depression. The oil is also effective for treating muscular aches and pains and arthritis.

On an emotional level, vetiver promotes wisdom, self-esteem, healing, balance, and a centered, calm approach to dealing with difficult situations. It's a good all-around oil for protection from negative energy and for fostering peaceful and loving feelings.

Vetiver also promotes restful sleep and pleasant dreams—try using it in a diffuser, in a blend with lavender or on its own, in your bedroom an hour or so before turning in for the night.

Magically, vetiver oil has a diverse range of applications. It has been used in spellwork and rituals relating to balance and grounding, as well as money, love, sex, protection from theft, and reversal of hexes.

One simple shielding method is to inhale the aroma while visualizing a bubble of white light surrounding you, insulating you from all negativity.

You can do this from the bottle or with a few drops in an oil burner or diffuser.

Use vetiver to anoint candles, charms, or actual money to attract more cash into your life. For even stronger results, use the inhalation method to visualize having more money before doing the actual spellwork.

Add vetiver oil to love sachets, bathwater, or a body blend to attract new potential lovers. For dealing with a string of bad luck, try adding a drop to a raw incense blend. For achieving balance in a situation that has been complicated by negative emotions, use 5-7 drops in a bath along with sea salt to clear away old, unwanted energy and make way for positive progress.

Vetiver's deep, woody, refreshing scent blends well with tree oils like cedarwood and sandalwood, florals like rose, geranium, and ylang ylang, earthy scents like patchouli and lavender, and citrus oils like bergamot and lemon.

Magical Associations:

Element: Earth
Planet: Saturn, Mercury, Venus
Zodiac: Cancer, Leo, Capricorn, Aquarius
Deities: Aphrodite/Venus, Pan

YLANG YLANG
(CANANGA ODORATA)

Although the name "ylang ylang" is translated from the Philippine language of Tagalog to mean "flower of flowers," the plant that this oil is extracted from is actually a tree.

The ylang ylang tree is native to several islands in Southeast Asia, where it is valued for its bark and leaves as well as the masses of fragrant flowers that bloom continually throughout the year. Its glossy leaves have been used in these tropical cultures to heal skin conditions, while the bark is used to treat a range of issues from pneumonia to ulcers.

The greenish-yellow flowers are widely used for malaria, asthma, and stomach problems, in addition to being distilled to make the essential oil. In Indonesia, the petals are strewn over the bed of newlyweds to enhance sensuality and romance.

In the West, ylang ylang is a valued ingredient in several high-end women's fragrances, and has becoming quite popular in many skin and hair care products.

The process of making the oil involves several stages of distillation, and the oil produced from each stage is usually sold separately. Many manufacturers identify their products with labels like "ylang ylang 1," and "ylang ylang 2," as well as "ylang ylang extra" or "superior," and even "ylang ylang complete."

The "complete" version contains oil from each of the stages of distillation, and is valued by aromatherapists for having the full spectrum of essential oil compounds. Ylang ylang extra (also known as "superior") is the oil resulting from the first distillation, and the subsequent rounds are identified as 1, 2, and so on. "Extra" is the headiest, sweetest scent, with each subsequent distillation producing a milder version.

If you buy an oil that is simply called "ylang ylang," it is probably made from the second or third distillation. Ideally, you can try different tester bottles to find which version you like best, but for the purposes of spellwork, it really doesn't matter.

In addition to the traditional uses in its native lands, ylang ylang oil is used to address high blood pressure, impotence and depression. It is a powerful sedative that can induce euphoria and is considered to have a narcotic effect when used in large quantities.

On the emotional level, the energy of ylang ylang helps to quell anger and frustration and transform negative emotions into positive energy. It is a good oil for those who struggle with self-love and self-forgiveness, clearing up space to attract more joy and enthusiasm in daily life.

Magical uses for ylang ylang are largely centered on grounding, protection and clearing negativity as well as peace, sex and love. It can be a powerful aphrodisiac, but be sparing with the oil at first, as it can be overpowering and even cause headaches or nausea if too much is used.

For creating sexual desire, add it to a blend with rose or palmarosa or use it singly to anoint your pulse points. Use it in charms aimed at manifesting love or peace. Place a drop or two in a diffuser or burner to create a positive, loving atmosphere in your home or sacred space. You can also wear the scent to help you stay calm through potentially stressful situations like a job interview or a public performance.

Due to the various versions of the oil produced from the distillation process, ylang ylang oil is said to be highly susceptible to adulteration, meaning that lesser quality versions may be sold as "complete" or "superior" oils. To reduce your chances of getting a falsely labeled bottle, be sure to research the reputation of the supplier before purchasing.

Although the degree of sweetness and other aspects of the oil may vary from brand to brand, ylang ylang is always a strong floral scent with a fresh, slightly fruity quality. It blends well with other florals like jasmine, neroli and rose, citrus oils like bergamot, lemon and orange, and select other oils including patchouli, sandalwood, vetiver and palmarosa.

Magical Associations:

Element: Earth, Water
Planet: Saturn, Venus
Zodiac: Aries, Taurus, Scorpio
Deities: Aphrodite, Persephone, Demeter

LET THE BLENDING BEGIN

Hopefully, at least a few of these delightful oils have caught your eye. And now that you know how to purchase and store them with confidence, you're ready to start making some magic!

Part Three provides basic blending instructions and recipes, along with spells and ideas for incorporating oils into your practice in a variety of ways. The spells and recipes call for oils from the Witch's dozen described above, but you can generally substitute other oils that resonate with you more on a personal level, if you wish. So read on for a "mini-grimoire" of ideas and advice for working your own oil magic.

PART THREE

PUTTING IT ALL TOGETHER

BLENDS, SPELLS, AND OTHER WAYS TO USE BOTANICAL OILS

In this section, you'll find thorough instructions for the blending process, eleven recipe ideas to get your practice going, and a few spells and other ideas for using your newly-created blends.

A table of correspondence with magical properties and associations follows at the end of the guide for easy reference as you chart your own course in using oils in magic.

CREATING YOUR BLENDS

Like any other aspect of magic, creating the perfect magical blends takes experimentation and practice. But with persistence, the right equipment and a few example recipes, you'll be a successful alchemist of botanical oils in short order!

CHOOSING A CARRIER OIL

Most sources on blending oils list the following carrier oils as options for your blends: safflower, sunflower, coconut, apricot kernel, jojoba, almond, hazelnut, grape seed, sweet almond, and macadamia nut.

This list represents a wide variety of color, scent and consistency, so these oils should not be considered interchangeable.

The best oil for you may depend on various factors: your intended use for the oil, your magical aim, and your personal preference.

If you are already familiar with a few of these oils from cooking experience, this is an advantage, as you'll have a feel for their color, relative weight, and scent (or lack thereof).

If you're brand-new to oils in general, try starting with safflower or grape seed, as these are fairly light and don't give off a noticeable scent, which will allow you to focus on the scents of your essential oils.

Jojoba is a popular oil among Witches and aromatherapists alike and has a heavier consistency. However, it's not really a cooking oil, so if you're budget-conscious and wanting to be practical, a culinary oil is probably a better bet.

On the other end of the spectrum is coconut oil, which has advantages and disadvantages. If you're making oil to anoint candles with, coconut holds well to the wax (as does jojoba).

However, it solidifies in cooler temperatures and has a strong, though delightful, scent. Depending on which essential oils you're using, this could be a mismatch, so avoid thinking of coconut oil as an all-purpose carrier.

Olive oil will also work in a pinch, but is prized more for its benefits to the skin than to its suitability for blending scents. Other carriers recommended for use on skin, whether for ritual anointing or magical fragrances, include apricot kernel and safflower oil.

BLENDING SUPPLIES

You really don't need a ton of equipment for blending botanical oils. However, you do need to use the *right* equipment, or you'll end up with blends of substandard quality. Don't make the mistake of thinking plastic will serve as a substitute for glass, and be sure that all of your equipment is squeaky clean before you begin!

To create truly potent and long-lasting magical blends, you'll need the following:

- Essential oils to blend

- Carrier oil

- Clean sterilized glass jar for mixing

- Small funnel(s) for transferring your blends

- Small blue or brown glass bottle with lids for storing your blends

- Small glass droppers (or disposable pipettes) for using your blends in spellwork (and for oils that don't come with single-drop dispensers)

To sterilize your mixing jars, wash them with dish soap in hot water and rinse them thoroughly. Make sure there are no traces of food or other residue inside or out. Wash the lids thoroughly as well.

Place the jars in a deep pot of water and cover with water—there should be an inch of water above the top of the jar. Bring the water to a rolling boil and leave it boiling for 10 minutes.

Turn off the heat, allow the pot to cool for a few minutes, and remove the jars with tongs. Pour any water out and let the jars cool to room temperature. Dry them thoroughly before using—you don't want any moisture diluting your oils.

Glass droppers, small bottles and funnels are available online, and often at health food stores and other retail shops where essential oils are sold. These supplies are usually very inexpensive. Be sure your small glass bottles come with screw-top caps rather than the dual-purpose glass dropper caps, unless you're going to use all of your blend over the course of a few weeks. Some manufacturers sell these bottles with the single-drop orifice reducers as well.

Many people like to reuse their bottles from blend to blend, which is fine as long as you clean them properly. Start by rinsing the bottles, caps, and droppers in cold water, then soak them in vinegar for 10-20 minutes. Then rinse with hot water, and soak in hot soapy water for another 10-20 minutes. Rinse and allow to dry thoroughly before using again.

As for reusing glass droppers, this can be a bit trickier. While some oils will dissolve in the vinegar/soapy water process, others—patchouli and vanilla in particular—are notoriously hard to completely remove from the inside of the dropper. (If you see any traces of water inside the dropper after everything else is dry, there is most likely still oil there.)

One option is to label droppers for use with one specific oil only, though this means you can't use them with a blend.

Some people choose to forego the glass droppers altogether and use disposable plastic pipettes instead. This is entirely up to you!

A NOTE ON PROPORTIONS

Although the process of creating essential oils involves a high degree of attention to detail, the work of blending them is not at all an exact science.

Different sources will give you sometimes very different recommendations for how much essential oil should be added to the carrier oil in a standard blend. Some say 7-10 drops per ounce of carrier oil is ideal, while others say 15-20.

So how do you know how many drops to use? The real answer is to experiment and learn your own preferences as you go. For the time being, however, you can keep a few guidelines in mind:

- **Potency:** some oils, like peppermint and ylang ylang, have particularly powerful scents, so you may want to go easy on them until you've tried them in a few blends. Simply give the uncapped bottle a gentle sniff to get a sense of how strong it is before deciding how many drops to use.

- **Sensitivity:** we all have different reactions to essential oils. If any given oil seems particularly potent to you, it's a good idea to ease up on it in a blend until you know how much you can tolerate. And if you don't like the scent of it at all, then you probably don't want to work with it at all!

- **Purpose:** if the oil is to be used on skin, even just for anointing purposes, you may want to err on the side of a "weak" blend until you know how your skin will react to the individual ingredients. This is especially true of cinnamon, clove, and any other oils that are potential skin irritants.

You can find plenty of more detailed information about proportions and creating blends, particularly from aromatherapy sources. But it's also fine to simply experiment on your own, and embrace the role of the 21st century alchemist!

Just be sure to keep track of what you're doing, so that when you hit on a combination you really like, you can write it down and recreate it again in the future.

BASIC BLENDING PROCESS

Find a flat surface to work on—usually a kitchen counter or table is best, for easy clean-up in the event of spills— and assemble all of the necessary supplies.

If you like, include a candle in your work space and light it with the intention that your creation will be powerful and successful. Play some calming or uplifting music—something that puts you in a relaxed and creative state of mind. If you feel called to do so, ask any guides or helpers in the spiritual realm to assist you in your work.

Though these steps are purely optional, it can be very helpful to create a magical state of mind as you begin your blending. You'll find that the process goes more smoothly and is more enjoyable!

But no matter how you begin, be sure that you've spent some time deciding on and then visualizing your magical goal(s) for the blend. The clearer you are on what you're looking to achieve, the more likely your success will be.

If you're making a general, all-purpose anointing oil for ritual, you might just focus on a vision of yourself in perfect harmony with the God and Goddess as you place the soon-to-be-manifested blend on your wrists and third eye. If your goal is to attract love or money, call up the feelings you want to feel when you've achieved success. If you're making a blend for a specific spell, such as one for landing a job, you can fine-tune your intention-setting even further by visualizing the results with specific detail.

But no matter what your purpose is, the most important thing is to keep your energy positive as you create your magical oil.

When you feel focused and ready, measure out the carrier oil and pour it into the mixing jar. For a standard batch of blended oil, use 1/8 cup (or 2 tablespoons) of carrier.

Close your eyes and take a long, deep breath. Now you're ready to add the first essential oil of the recipe.

Using an eyedropper or the single-drop dispenser included in most essential oil bottles, count out the amount of drops called for in the recipe. Be sure to follow the order the ingredients are listed in, as the larger amounts should go into the blend first (follow this guideline when inventing your own blends, as well).

Gently swirl the jar around clockwise to mix the oil into the carrier. Sniff the jar as you close your eyes and once again visualize your goal.

Add the next oil and swirl the jar clockwise again. Sniff and notice the difference the second oil has made to the scent of the blend.

Close your eyes as you inhale and visualize your goal. Repeat this process with each additional essential oil in the recipe, swirling, sniffing and visualizing as the energies of the plants mingle together in your magical concoction.

The objective is to let the scents become associated with the vision of the goal in your mind as you create the blend. Then when you use the oil in your spellwork, the vibrational energy of the plants will combine with the energy of your vision to manifest the goal on the physical plane.

As you become more familiar with various oils, you will no doubt develop preferences for certain scents, and you may want to adjust proportions in the recipes that you work with. Don't be afraid to experiment with this as you create your blends—try adding a drop or two more of any given oil in a recipe to tailor the overall scent to your liking.

When you feel the blend is complete, use a funnel to transfer it from the mixing jar to a small glass bottle. Cap the bottle and label it with the name of the blend.

Don't forget the crucial step of charging your newly-blended magical oil! Hold the bottle in your hands and send your personal energy into the oil by focusing once again on your goal. If you have a charging ritual, such as invoking the Goddess and God, perform that now.

Then store your oil in a cool, dark place until it's time to use it in your spellwork.

OIL BLEND RECIPES

The following recipes can be used for anointing your altar, ritual tools, talismans, crystals and spell ingredients, and can be active ingredients themselves in spellwork.

Keep in mind, this is just a brief sample of the vast range of possibilities for blends. The proportions listed are merely suggestions—again, it's good to experiment with specific amounts until you find the combinations you like best.

Lucky Money Oil:

- 5 drops patchouli
- 4 drops bergamot
- 2 drops cedarwood
- 1 drop lavender

Love Energy Oil:

- 5 drops rose
- 3 drops patchouli
- 2 drops ylang ylang
- 2 drops vetiver

Hearth and Home Protection Oil:

- 5 drops vetiver
- 3 drops cinnamon
- 2 drops clove
- 1 drop ylang ylang

Happy Healing Oil:

- 5 drops palmarosa
- 4 drops cedarwood
- 4 drops lemon
- 2 drops lavender

Higher Self Oil:

- 5 drops juniper
- 4 drops palmarosa
- 3 drops bergamot

Purification Oil 1:

- 5 drops juniper
- 3 drops cedarwood
- 1 drop lavender

Purification Oil 2:

- 5 drops peppermint
- 3 drops clove
- 2 drops lemon

Earth Element Oil:

- 4 drops patchouli
- 3 drops rose
- 2 drops vetiver

Air Element Oil:

- 5 drops bergamot
- 3 drops lavender
- 3 drops peppermint

Fire Element Oil:

- 5 drops cinnamon
- 3 drops clove
- 2 drops rose

Water Element Oil:

- 6 drops lemon
- 3 drops palmarosa
- 2 drops ylang ylang

OIL-FOCUSED SPELLWORK

The following spells draw heavily on the power of blended oils, by using them in multiple ways.

First, you'll anoint your body, signaling the summoning of your personal power. Then you'll anoint a candle, connecting your personal power to that of the Element of Fire. The third use of the oil is where these spells really differ—one calls for the anointing of coins, another for the inclusion of oil in a charm bag, and the third uses steam to bring the power of the oil into full force throughout your magical space.

COINS AND CANDLE MONEY SPELL

Coins make for good magical tools for prosperity, not only because they are literal representations of wealth, but because they can also symbolize the seeds of future wealth to come. When you add the focused energies of your own *Lucky Money Oil*, the spell becomes even more powerful!

At each stage of the spell, it's important that you behave as if you have already received the money. Spend a few minutes imagining the feeling of receiving money unexpectedly. Perhaps you can recall a time when you found a dollar on the ground or got a surprise check in the mail. If you can't recall any specific event, invent one and imagine it in detail.

Feel the gratitude and excitement that comes with discovering unexpected money, and channel this energy into the magical work.

You will need:

- Lucky Money Oil
- 1 green candle
- 3 quarters (or dollar coins, if you have them)
- Crystal point, athame, or other ritual carving tool

Instructions:

First, anoint your temples, third eye, and pulse points with the oil.

Then inscribe your initials on the candle along with a symbol of money—a dollar sign, for example, or a rune associated with wealth.

Hold it in your hands for a few moments and visualize your personal power flowing into the candle itself.

When you feel ready, anoint it with the Lucky Money Oil and place it in its holder.

Next, hold the coins stacked together between your palms.

Again, summon the feeling of happy surprise at receiving an unexpected boon to your finances.

Arrange the coins, face up, in the shape of a triangle around the candle, with the top point of the triangle facing you.

Anoint them with the oil by placing one drop on the center of each coin, saying these (or your own) words three times: *"As like attracts like, this money brings more."*

Now, as you light the candle, say *"So let it be."*

Allow the candle to burn out on its own before removing the coins.

Place one in your kitchen, one in your living area, and carry the third with you in your purse, wallet, or the pocket of some item of clothing that you wear daily.

In the days after you work this spell, be careful not to try to figure out where the extra money will come from, lest you get in the way of the magic. Money can come from all kinds of unexpected places.

Go about your usual routine, and trust that you will see the results of the spell when the time is right.

If you like, open your Lucky Money Oil blend from time to time and inhale its scent, to bring back the positive feelings you experienced while working the spell.

THEFT PROTECTION CHARM

This charm is best for use in your home—whether it be a bedroom, dorm room, or an entire house—but can also be placed in your car if you like.

You will need:

- Hearth and Home Protection Oil
- 1 black spell candle
- 1 bay leaf
- 1 pinch each of dried basil and nutmeg
- 1 amethyst or clear quartz crystal
- 1 drawstring charm sachet

Instructions:

Anoint your temples, third eye, and pulse points with the oil.

Then anoint the candle while visualizing your environment encircled and infused with white light.

Place the crystal in the charm bag, followed by the herbs.

Sprinkle 3 drops of the oil into the bag, then pull it closed.

Light the candle and place the charm in front of it, while saying the following (or your own) words:

"Through herbs, stone and oil
Would-be thieves this charm does foil.
So let it be."

Leave the charm in place until the candle has burned out.

Then place it somewhere in your home where it will not draw unnecessary attention, but you will still see it.

STEAMY LOVE ATTRACTION SPELL

This spell is suitable for both singles and people in relationships looking to spice up their love life. The chief crystalizing action of the spell is actually the pouring of the water onto the essential oils.

If possible, use just the single oils called for in the *Love Energy* blend, rather than the blend itself, for the diffusing step. Otherwise, you can use the blend for the diffusing step, but it's not as aromatically satisfying due to the mix of water and carrier oil.

Be sure that the water is not actually boiling when you pour it, or you'll scorch the oil. If it reaches a boil before you take it off the stove, let it sit and cool for a minute before pouring.

This should go without saying, but be very careful not to aim your energy at a specific person in a manipulative way. This can really backfire, even if you have your partner or spouse in mind. It's never wise to concentrate on controlling the feelings or actions of another—instead, concentrate on how *you* want to feel in the experience you're manifesting.

You will need:

- 1 red spell candle
- Love Energy Oil for anointing

- Single vials of rose, patchouli, ylang ylang and vetiver for diffusing (optional)
- 1 cup of filtered water
- Tea, kettle, or small sauce pan
- Cauldron, or other non-metallic bowl not used for food
- Pinch of dried lavender, patchouli, and/or hibiscus

Instructions:

Take a few moments to call up memories and feelings of well-being, excitement, and physical attraction. How do you feel when you're caught up in the energy of a passionate love affair? Concentrate on that delightful thrill as you anoint your wrists, pulse points, and third eye with the oil.

Hold the cup of water in your hands and charge it with the energy of love and passion.

Next, pour the water into the kettle or pan and put it on the stove to boil. (Don't use a microwave unless you absolutely have to.)

While the water heats, anoint the candle and sprinkle the herbs in a circle around its base.

Continuing to visualize your goal, light the candle and say these (or your own) words:

"Love and passion,
in my own fashion,
I call to me
through power of attraction."

When the water is just about to boil, take it off the heat. Then place 1-2 drops each of the single essential oils (or 6-8 drops of the full Love Energy blend) in the cauldron or bowl.

Set it on your altar or other heat-resistant work space.

Gently pour the water over the oil, while repeating the words above and then ending with *"So let it be."*

Now step back a bit from the cauldron, as the scent of the volatile oils will be quite strong at first.

Visualize your personal power carried on the steam as it rises up and crosses into the non-physical planes of the Universe.

Wait until the water has cooled and most of the scent has evaporated before pouring it out.

Allow the candle to burn all the way down on its own. The faster it burns, the sooner your love experience will come into your life!

TAKING IT FURTHER

There are so many more options for using essential oils in your magic. Here are just three popular practices that are simple, elegant, and beginner friendly:

- Use essential oils to create your own ritual bath salts. You can use many of the combinations in the recipes above (just avoid blends with known skin irritants). In place of the carrier oil, use epsom salts, baking soda and table salt.

- Add herbs and/or crystal chips to your oil blends for even more unique & magically potent blends. Use ingredients aligned with the intent of the oil. For example, a pinch of dried basil and a chip or two of citrine can be added to a money-related blend.

- In lieu of incense, enhance your sacred space with a few drops of essential oil in a tea-light burner or steam diffuser. Again, you can use the recipes above, but skip the carrier oil and reduce the total amount of drops to between 3 to 7 drops per 100ml of water.

CONCLUSION

The intention of this guide has been to provide you with a solid grounding in the use of botanical oils in magic. You now have enough knowledge to begin exploring on your own.

You can find plenty more recipes, spells and ideas in a wealth of sources in print and online. A few recommended books follow the table of correspondence at the end of this guide.

As always, use your intuition when choosing what to read and which oils to try out in your practice. And above all else, enjoy the process of discovery!

Blessed Be.

TABLES OF CORRESPONDENCE: BOTANICAL OILS

Essential Oil	Magical Uses	Element
Bergamot	Positive energy, confidence, success, prosperity, peace	Fire, Air
Cedarwood	Healing, rebirth, spirituality, hex reversal, banishing	Fire
Cinnamon	Psychic awareness, protection, healing, success, love	Fire
Clove	Protection, courage, wealth, purification, banishing	Fire
Juniper	Purification, protection, healing, love	Fire
Lavender	Healing, peace, love, wealth, purification, dissolving anxiety	Air
Lemon	Positive energy, healing, longevity, purification, spiritual awareness	Water
Palmarosa	Emotional healing, love, transitions, change	Water
Patchouli	Love, lust, physical energy, money, prosperity	Earth
Peppermint	Dreamwork, dissolving obstacles, purification	Earth, Air, Fire
Rose	Love, peace, balance, enhancing beauty	Earth, Water, Fire
Vetiver	Balance, grounding, love, protection from theft, hex reversal	Earth
Ylang Ylang	Grounding, protection, peace, sex, love	Earth, Water

Essential Oil	Planet	Zodiac Sign
Bergamot	Sun, Mercury	Gemini, Virgo
Cedarwood	Sun	Aries, Sagittarius
Cinnamon	Sun	Aries, Leo
Clove	Jupiter	Pisces, Scorpio, Sagittarius
Juniper	Sun, Jupiter	Aries, Leo, Sagittarius
Lavender	Mercury	Gemini, Virgo, Aquarius
Lemon	Moon	Pisces, Cancer
Palmarosa	Venus	Pisces, Cancer, Libra
Patchouli	Saturn	Taurus, Virgo, Capricorn, Sagittarius
Peppermint	Mercury, Mars	Aries, Gemini, Virgo, Aquarius
Rose	Saturn, Venus	Taurus, Cancer, Libra, Sagittarius
Vetiver	Saturn, Mercury, Venus	Cancer, Leo, Capricorn, Aquarius
Ylang Ylang	Saturn, Venus	Aries, Taurus, Scorpio

Essential Oil	Deities	Cautionary Notes*
Bergamot	Persephone, Fortuna, Hermes, Mercury	Skin-photosensitizing
Cedarwood	Pan, Aphrodite, Cernunnos, Artemis, Isis, Jupiter	Avoid during pregnancy
Cinnamon	Aphrodite/Venus, Demeter, Mercury, Bast, Ra, Brighid	Skin irritant, avoid during pregnancy
Clove	Osiris, Isis, Toth	Skin irritant, avoid during pregnancy
Juniper	Astarte/Ishtar, Pan, Brighid	Avoid during pregnancy
Lavender	Demeter, Cernunnos, Hecate, Saturn, Brighid	Avoid *lavandula stoechas* (French/Spanish variety) during pregnancy
Lemon	Athena, Diana, Luna, Neptune	Skin-photosensitizing
Palmarosa	Demeter, Athena	
Patchouli	Hecate, Pan, Aphrodite, Hestia	
Peppermint	Artemis, Hecate, Cernunnos	Avoid during pregnancy
Rose	Aphrodite/Venus, Demeter, Isis	
Vetiver	Aphrodite/Venus, Pan, Demeter	
Ylang Ylang	Aphrodite, Persephone, Demeter	

SUGGESTIONS FOR FURTHER READING

For some reason, there are not as many quality books focusing on oil magic out there as there are for other areas of Witchcraft. Instead, oils tend to be covered along with related topics, such as incense and herbal magic, in more all-encompassing books.

That being said, there is an explosion of resources related to aromatherapy, some of which are well-worth checking out for those interested in incorporating more direct healing work into their practice. After all, you can always use recipes from aromatherapy sources in your spellwork—with potentially astounding results!

To that end, books that don't hail directly from the magical realm are included on this list. Enjoy exploring the wide world of botanical oils!

Scott Cunningham, *Magical Aromatherapy: The Power of Scent* (1989)

Scott Cunningham, *The Complete Book of Incense, Oils & Brews* (1989)

Sandra Kynes, *Mixing Essential Oils for Magic: Aromatic Alchemy* (2013)

Carol Schiller and David Schiller, *500 Formulas for Aromatherapy: Mixing Essential Oils for Every Use* (1994)

Kurt Schnaubelt Ph.D., *The Healing Intelligence of Essential Oils: The Science of Advanced Aromatherapy* (2011)

Valeria Ann Worwood, *The Complete Book of Essential Oils & Aromatherapy* (1991)

THREE FREE AUDIOBOOKS PROMOTION

Don't forget, you can now enjoy **three audiobooks completely free of charge** when you start a free 30-day trial with Audible.

If you're new to the Craft, *Wicca Starter Kit* contains three of Lisa's most popular books for beginning Wiccans. You can download it for free at:

www.wiccaliving.com/free-wiccan-audiobooks

Or, if you're wanting to expand your magical skills, check out *Spellbook Starter Kit,* with three collections of spellwork featuring the powerful energies of candles, colors, crystals, mineral stones, and magical herbs. Download over 150 spells for free at:

www.wiccaliving.com/free-spell-audiobooks

Members receive free audiobooks every month, as well as exclusive discounts. And, if you don't want to continue with Audible, just remember to cancel your membership. You won't be charged a cent, and you'll get to keep your books!

Happy listening!

MORE BOOKS BY LISA CHAMBERLAIN

Wicca for Beginners: A Guide to Wiccan Beliefs, Rituals, Magic, and Witchcraft

Wicca Book of Spells: A Book of Shadows for Wiccans, Witches, and Other Practitioners of Magic

Wicca Herbal Magic: A Beginner's Guide to Practicing Wiccan Herbal Magic, with Simple Herb Spells

Wicca Book of Herbal Spells: A Book of Shadows for Wiccans, Witches, and Other Practitioners of Herbal Magic

Wicca Candle Magic: A Beginner's Guide to Practicing Wiccan Candle Magic, with Simple Candle Spells

Wicca Book of Candle Spells: A Book of Shadows for Wiccans, Witches, and Other Practitioners of Candle Magic

Wicca Crystal Magic: A Beginner's Guide to Practicing Wiccan Crystal Magic, with Simple Crystal Spells

Wicca Book of Crystal Spells: A Book of Shadows for Wiccans, Witches, and Other Practitioners of Crystal Magic

Tarot for Beginners: A Guide to Psychic Tarot Reading, Real Tarot Card Meanings, and Simple Tarot Spreads

Runes for Beginners: A Guide to Reading Runes in Divination, Rune Magic, and the Meaning of the Elder Futhark Runes

Wicca Moon Magic: A Wiccan's Guide and Grimoire for Working Magic with Lunar Energies

Wicca Wheel of the Year Magic: A Beginner's Guide to the Sabbats, with History, Symbolism, Celebration Ideas, and Dedicated Sabbat Spells

Wicca Kitchen Witchery: A Beginner's Guide to Magical Cooking, with Simple Spells and Recipes

Wicca Essential Oils Magic: A Beginner's Guide to Working with Magical Oils, with Simple Recipes and Spells

Wicca Elemental Magic: A Guide to the Elements, Witchcraft, and Magical Spells

Wicca Magical Deities: A Guide to the Wiccan God and Goddess, and Choosing a Deity to Work Magic With

Wicca Living a Magical Life: A Guide to Initiation and Navigating Your Journey in the Craft

Magic and the Law of Attraction: A Witch's Guide to the Magic of Intention, Raising Your Frequency, and Building Your Reality

Wicca Altar and Tools: A Beginner's Guide to Wiccan Altars, Tools for Spellwork, and Casting the Circle

Wicca Finding Your Path: A Beginner's Guide to Wiccan Traditions, Solitary Practitioners, Eclectic Witches, Covens, and Circles

Wicca Book of Shadows: A Beginner's Guide to Keeping Your Own Book of Shadows and the History of Grimoires

Modern Witchcraft and Magic for Beginners: A Guide to Traditional and Contemporary Paths, with Magical Techniques for the Beginner Witch

FREE GIFT REMINDER

Just a reminder that Lisa is giving away an exclusive, free spell book as a thank-you gift to new readers!

Little Book of Spells contains ten spells that are ideal for newcomers to the practice of magic, but are also suitable for any level of experience.

Read it on read on your laptop, phone, tablet, Kindle or Nook device by visiting:

www.wiccaliving.com/bonus

DID YOU ENJOY *WICCA ESSENTIAL OILS MAGIC?*

Thanks so much for reading this book! I know there are many great books out there about Wicca, so I really appreciate you choosing this one.

If you enjoyed the book, I have a small favor to ask—would you take a couple of minutes to leave a review for this book on Amazon?

Your feedback will help me to make improvements to this book, and to create even better ones in the future. It will also help me develop new ideas for books on other topics that might be of interest to you. Thanks in advance for your help!

CPSIA information can be obtained
at www.ICGtesting.com
Printed in the USA
BVHW061807230321
603273BV00004B/377